Hedgehog

By Ruth Owen

Educational Consultant:
Dee Reid

Tips for Reading with Your Child

- Set aside at least 10 to 15 minutes each day for reading.

- Find a quiet place to sit with no distractions. Turn off the TV, music and screens.

- Encourage your child to hold the book and turn the pages.

- Before reading begins, look at the pictures together and talk about what you see.

- If the reader gets stuck on a word, try reading to the end of the sentence. Often by reading the word in context, he or she will be able to figure out the unknown word. Looking at the pictures can help, too.

- Words shown in **bold** are explained in the glossary on pages 22–23.

Above all enjoy the time together and make reading fun!

Book Band Blue

For more information about hedgehogs go to:
www.rubytuesdaybooks.com/wildlifewatchers

What do you know about hedgehogs?

How can you tell an animal is a hedgehog?

- It has a prickly body.
- It has colourful feathers.
- It has a furry body.

What do hedgehogs eat?

- Seeds and berries
- Frogs and mice
- Worms and snails

What does a hedgehog do when it's scared?

- It curls up in a ball.
- It hisses and spits.
- It runs away.

What is a baby hedgehog called?

- A mini hog
- A hoglet
- A piglet

Now read this book and find the answers.

This mother hedgehog is looking for food.

snail

First, she finds a snail to eat.

worm

Then she finds a fat worm to eat.

Hedgehog Food

beetle   millipede   earwig   slug

When the hedgehog is full,
she goes home.

A dog sees the hedgehog.

He wants to play with her.

The hedgehog is scared of the dog.

She curls up into a prickly ball.

spines

Ouch!

The prickly **spines** hurt the dog's nose
so he runs away!

The hedgehog runs home to her **nest**.

The nest is under a shed.

Who is waiting in the nest?

Her babies are waiting in the nest.

The babies are called **hoglets**.

The tiny hoglets cannot see or hear.

a four-day-old hoglet

The hedgehog feeds her babies with milk from her body.

When they are two weeks old, the hoglets can see and hear.

When they are four weeks old, they go outside with their mother.

a four-week-old hoglet

The hoglets look for snails, worms
and slugs to eat.

When they are eight weeks old, the hoglets leave their mother to begin their grown-up life.

After her babies leave, the hedgehog lives alone.

Soon it is autumn.

She finds a **hollow** log for her winter nest.

The hedgehog makes a bed of leaves inside her nest.

Then she goes to sleep for the winter.

This long sleep is called **hibernation.**

See you in the spring!

Glossary

hibernation
Spending the winter in a deep sleep. Hibernating animals don't eat, but live off their body fat.

hoglet
A baby hedgehog.

hollow
Having an empty space inside. Not solid.

nest
An animal's home where it sleeps and takes care of its babies.

spine
A thin, sharp point that grows from a hedgehog's body.

Hedgehog Quiz

1 Where did the hedgehog live with her babies?

2 What food does a hedgehog feed to her babies?

3 How old is a hoglet when it leaves its mother?

4 How does a hedgehog spend the winter?

5 Can you guess how many spines are on a hedgehog's body?

(The answer is at the bottom of the page.)

Answer Question 5:
A hedgehog has about 7000 spines on its body.